ALGEBRA
LINEAR EQUATIONS

WORKBOOK

Acknowledgements

The author and publisher are grateful to the copyright holders for permission to use quoted materials and images.

Published by Inspire Studies.

ISBN 9798848554267

First published in 2022

All rights reserved. No part of this publication may be reproduced, stored in a retrieval system or transmitted in any form or by any means, electronic, mechanical, photocopying, recording or otherwise, without the prior permission of Inspire Studies. The publisher has made every effort to trace and contact all copyright holders before publication; however, this has not been possible in all cases. If notified, the publisher will rectify any errors or omissions at the earliest opportunity.

Author: Teresa Maine
Editor: Gordon Goulding
Cover Design: Roman Derkach
Proof reading by Proofed.

Copyright ©2022 Inspire Studies

Contents

1. The Balance Method for Solving Linear Equations — 4
2. Solving Linear Equations by Working Backwards — 10
3. Solving Equations with Brackets — 13
4. Linear Equations with Unknown Letters on Both Sides — 20
5. Linear Equations with Fractional Terms — 27
6. Setting Up and Solving Linear Equations — 35

Answers — 42

ALGEBRA LINEAR EQUATIONS

1. The Balance Method for Solving Linear Equations

Example :

Use the balance method to solve the equation $5x + 23 = 48$

Solution :

$5x + 23 = 48$

$5x + 23 - 23 = 48 - 23$ Subtract 23 from both sides.

$5x = 25$

$\dfrac{5x}{5} = \dfrac{25}{5}$ Divide both sides by 5.

$x = 5$

Example :

Use the balance method to solve the equation $4n - 8 = 24$

Solution :

$4n - 8 + 8 = 24 + 8$ Add 8 to both sides.

$4n = 32$

$\dfrac{4n}{4} = \dfrac{32}{4}$ Divide both sides by 4.

$n = 8$

ALGEBRA LINEAR EQUATIONS

Example :

Use the balance method to solve the equation $\dfrac{1}{3}d - 5 = 16$

Solution :

$\dfrac{1}{3}d - 5 + 5 = 16 + 5$ Add 5 to both sides.

$\dfrac{1}{3}d = 21$

$\cancel{3} \times \dfrac{1}{\cancel{3}}d = 21 \times 3$ Multiply both sides by 3 and cancel the terms.

$d = 63$

Example :

Use the balance method to solve the equation $\dfrac{3}{5}d - \dfrac{1}{3} = 5$

Solution :

$\cancel{15}^{5} \times \dfrac{1}{\cancel{3}^{1}}d - \cancel{15}^{3} \times \dfrac{1}{\cancel{5}^{1}} = 5 \times 15$ Multiply each side by 15 and cancel the terms.

$5d - 3 = 75$

$5d - 3 + 3 = 75 + 3$ Add 3 to both sides.

$5d = 78$

$\dfrac{5d}{5} = \dfrac{78}{5}$ Divide both sides by 5.

$d = \dfrac{78}{5} = 15\dfrac{3}{5}$

ALGEBRA LINEAR EQUATIONS

Exercise 1:

1. Solve these equations using the balance method. Do not use a calculator.

(a) $2a = 18$

(b) $4x = 10$

(c) $12m = 24$

(d) $6y = 48$

(e) $5n = 30$

(f) $7b = 28$

2. Solve these equations using the balance method. Do not use a calculator.

(a) $-5b = 35$

(b) $-4u = 18$

(c) $-21d = 36$

ALGEBRA LINEAR EQUATIONS

(d) $-30g = 135$

(e) $-13m = 65$

(f) $-16y = 8$

3. Solve these equations using the balance method.

(a) $4y + 8 = -8$

(b) $-6p - 3 = 15$

(c) $5m + 23 = -2$

(d) $3 + 6g = -15$

(e) $-2 - 4n = 26$

(f) $-7 - 3n = 17$

ALGEBRA LINEAR EQUATIONS

4. Solve these equations using the balance method.

(a) $y + 3 = -11$

(b) $t - 5 = -6$

(c) $6 - n = 8$

(d) $m + 3 = 6$

(e) $8 - p = -3$

(f) $12 - q = -4$

ALGEBRA LINEAR EQUATIONS

5. Solve each of the following equations.

(a) $\dfrac{1}{2}g - 5 = 7$

(b) $\dfrac{2}{3}a + 5 = 15$

(c) $\dfrac{1}{4}b - 2 = 12$

(d) $\dfrac{3}{4}y + 6 = -6$

(e) $\dfrac{2}{5}d + 3 = 21$

(f) $\dfrac{3}{5}t - 2 = 13$

ALGEBRA LINEAR EQUATIONS

2. Solving Linear Equations by Working Backwards

Example :

Kevin thinks of a number. He adds 2, then multiplies it by 3. The answer is 18. Find the number.

Solution :

Let the number Kevin thinks of be x:

$x \longrightarrow \boxed{+2} \longrightarrow \boxed{\times 3} \longrightarrow 18$

$x = 2 \longleftarrow \boxed{-2} \longleftarrow 6 \longleftarrow \boxed{\div 3} \longleftarrow 18$

Example :

Joanna had £x in her bank account on Monday.

She withdrew £35 on Tuesday and received a weekly wage of £365.

She paid £420 for her rent and spent £180 on food shopping on Thursday.

Her balance is £1,325 on Friday.

Work out how much money Joanna had on Monday.

Solution :

Work backwards to find the initial amount.
$x = £1325 + £180 + £420 - £365 + £35 = £1595$

ALGEBRA LINEAR EQUATIONS

Exercise 2 :

Solve each of these problems by working backwards.

1. Angela thinks of a number. She divides it by 3 and then adds 5. The answer is 21. What is her number?

2. Wendy thinks of a number. She multiplies it by 5 and then divides it by 2. She adds 3, and the answer is 8. What is the number?

3. Jane is 5 years older than Ellen. Ellen is 12 years younger than Ian. If Jane is 42, how old is Ian?

ALGEBRA LINEAR EQUATIONS

4. Sharon plans to visit Scotland. She needs 25 minutes to get ready, and it takes her 15 minutes to walk to the train station. She likes to be on the platform 10 minutes before the train departs. If the train departs at 9:15, what time should Sharon leave home?

5. Use the function machine to write a formula for y in terms of x?

6. The number in each box below is the product of the numbers in the 2 boxes that touch it in the row above. Find the value of x and y.

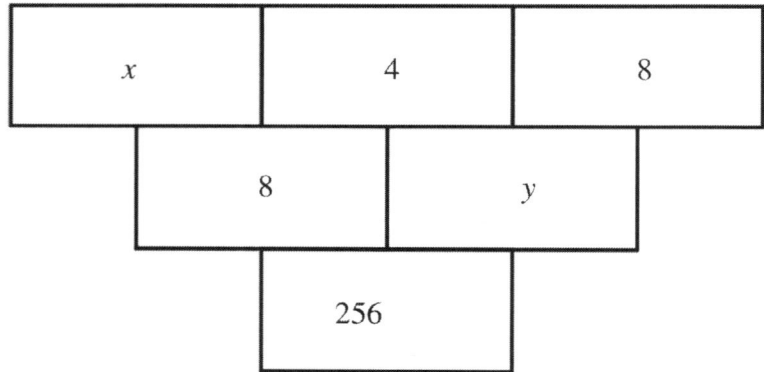

ALGEBRA LINEAR EQUATIONS

3. Solving Equations with Brackets

Example :

$3(2x + 3) = 33$

Solution :

$3(2x + 3) = 33$

$6x + 9 = 33$ Expand the bracket.

$6x + 9 - 9 = 33 - 9$ Subtract 9 from both sides.

$6x = 24$

$\dfrac{6x}{6} = \dfrac{24}{6}$ Divide both sides by 6.

$x = 4$

Example :

$4(p + 3) + 11 = 20$

Solution :

$4(p + 3) + 11 = 20$

$4p + 12 + 11 = 20$ Expand the bracket.

$4p + 23 = 20$ Simplify the equation.

$4p = -3$ Subtract 23 from both sides.

$p = -\dfrac{3}{4}$ Divide both sides by 4.

©Inspire Studies

ALGEBRA LINEAR EQUATIONS

Example :

$$-\frac{4}{3}(6y - 9) = 2$$

Solution :

$$-\frac{4}{3} \times 6y + 9 \times \frac{4}{3} = 2 \qquad \text{Expand the bracket.}$$

$$-\frac{4}{\cancel{3}^1} \times \cancel{6}^2 y + \cancel{9}^3 \times \frac{4}{\cancel{3}^1} = 2 \qquad \text{Cancel the terms and simplify.}$$

$$-8y + 12 = 2$$

$$-8y + 12 - 12 = 2 - 12 \qquad \text{Subtract 12 from both sides.}$$

$$-8y = -10$$

$$\frac{-8y}{-8} = \frac{-10}{-8} \qquad \text{Divide both sides by } -8.$$

$$y = \frac{5}{4} = 1\frac{1}{4}$$

Exercise 3 :

1. Solve the following equations.

(a) $2(3a + 5) = 28$

(b) $3(4a - 2) = 42$

©Inspire Studies

ALGEBRA LINEAR EQUATIONS

(c) $5(3a + 3) = 60$

(d) $7(2a - 13) = 7$

(e) $4(6a + 2) = 5$

(f) $3(5a - 3) = 21$

2. Solve the following equations.

(a) $-2(y - 3) = 5$

(b) $-3(y - 4) = 2$

(c) $-5(y - 3) = 4$

ALGEBRA LINEAR EQUATIONS

(d) $-3(y-2) = 8$

(e) $-3(2y-3) = 6$

(f) $-4(5y-6) = 8$

3. Solve the following equations.

(a) $\dfrac{1}{2}(6y+2) = -3$

(b) $\dfrac{1}{3}(3y+6) = -5$

(c) $\dfrac{2}{3}(9y+3) = -6$

ALGEBRA LINEAR EQUATIONS

(d) $\dfrac{3}{4}(12y + 16) = -6$

(e) $\dfrac{2}{5}(10y + 25) = -14$

(f) $\dfrac{4}{7}(21y + 14) = -4$

4. Solve the following equations.

(a) $-2(2b - 3) = 4$

(b) $-11(3b - 5) = 11$

(c) $-6(4b - 2) = 36$

(d) $-5(3b-7) = 25$

(e) $-2(13b-5) = -3$

(f) $-4(16b-5) = -36$

5. Solve for x

(a) $-\dfrac{1}{3}(9x-27) = -12$

(b) $-\dfrac{4}{5}(15x-20) = -8$

(c) $-\dfrac{3}{7}(21x-35) = -3$

ALGEBRA LINEAR EQUATIONS

(d) $-\dfrac{2}{5}(20x - 30) = -36$

(e) $-\dfrac{2}{9}(45x - 9) = -18$

(f) $-\dfrac{2}{3}(6x - 3) = -10$

(g) $-\dfrac{4}{7}(14x - 7) = 6$

(h) $-\dfrac{5}{9}(27x - 18) = 40$

ALGEBRA LINEAR EQUATIONS

4. Equations with Unknown Letters on Both Sides

Example :

$2n + 3 = 4n + 17$

Solution :

$2n + 3 = 4n + 17$

$2n + 3 - 4n - 3 = 4n + 17 - 4n - 3$ Subtract 3 and $4n$ from both sides.

$-2n = 14$

$\dfrac{-2n}{-2} = \dfrac{14}{-2}$ Divide both sides by -2.

$n = -7$

Example :

$6(3 + 4n) = 8(n + 3)$

Solution :

$18 + 24n = 8n + 24$ Expand the brackets on both sides.

$18 + 24n - 8n = 8n + 24 - 8n$ Subtract $8n$ from both sides and simplify.

$18 + 16n = 24$ Subtract 18 from both side and simplify.

$16n = 6$ Divide both sides by 16.

$n = \dfrac{3}{8}$

ALGEBRA LINEAR EQUATIONS

Exercise 4:

1. Solve the following equations.

(a) $4(2x + 6) = 3(4x + 5)$

(b) $2(3x + 2) = 3(5x + 4)$

(c) $6(3x + 5) = 3(2x + 1)$

(d) $7(2x + 4) = 6(3x + 8)$

(e) $8(4x + 3) = 6(5x + 2)$

(f) $9(2x + 3) = 5(3x + 6)$

ALGEBRA LINEAR EQUATIONS

2. Solve the following equations.

(a) $3(2a - 6) = 2(4a - 2)$

(b) $4(2a - 3) = 3(5a - 3)$

(c) $5(3a - 4) = 4(3a - 7)$

(d) $7(4a - 5) = 6(3a - 6)$

(e) $4(3a - 6) = 2(5a - 7)$

(f) $8(3a - 7) = 3(2a - 5)$

ALGEBRA LINEAR EQUATIONS

3. Solve the following equations.

(a) $4d - 5 = 6 + d$

(b) $3d - 4 = d + 9$

(c) $5d + 3 = 15 + d$

(d) $d + 6 = 3d + 2$

(e) $6d - 11 = 5d + 6$

(f) $4d + 1 = 13 - 2d$

ALGEBRA LINEAR EQUATIONS

4. Solve the following equations.

(a) $5m - 2 = 4(m + 2)$

(b) $2m - 11 = 3(3m - 5)$

(c) $3m + 7 = 2(2m - 2)$

(d) $9m - 3 = 5(3m + 3)$

(e) $6m - 4 = 7(4m - 5)$

(f) $5m - 6 = 3(m - 6)$

ALGEBRA LINEAR EQUATIONS

5. Solve the following equations.

(a) $4(x + 3) + 2(3x - 1) = 6(x - 5)$

(b) $2(x + 2) + 4(3x + 2) = 7(4x - 6)$

(c) $4(x - 3) - 2(3x + 3) = 5(x - 6)$

(d) $7(2x + 6) + 2(3x + 1) = -11(x - 2)$

(e) $-3(2x - 4) - 4(2x - 3) = -3(x - 11)$

(f) $5(3x - 4) + 2(6x + 4) = 12(x + 4)$

ALGEBRA LINEAR EQUATIONS

6. Solve the following equations.

(a) $2(y + 2) + 25 = 57$

(b) $3(y + 5) + 16 = 43$

(c) $5(y + 4) + 12 = 62$

(d) $6(y + 3) + 14 = 68$

(e) $11(2y - 3) - 6 = 32$

(f) $7(3y - 2) - 8 = 22$

ALGEBRA LINEAR EQUATIONS

5. Equations with Fractional Terms

Example :

$$\frac{4}{15}x = -2$$

Solution :

$$\cancel{15}^1 \times \frac{4}{\cancel{15}^1}x = -2 \times 15 \quad \text{Multiply both sides by 15 and cancel terms.}$$

$$4x = -30$$

$$x = -\frac{30}{4} \qquad \text{Divide both sides by 4 and simplify.}$$

$$x = -\frac{15}{2} = -7\frac{1}{2}$$

Example :

$$\frac{x+1}{2} = 5$$

Solution :

$$\frac{x+1}{\cancel{2}^1} \times \cancel{2}^1 = 5 \times 2 \quad \text{Multiply both sides by 2 and cancel terms.}$$

$$x + 1 = 10 \qquad \text{Subtract 1 from both sides.}$$

$$x = 9$$

ALGEBRA LINEAR EQUATIONS

Exercise 5:

1. Solve the following equations.

(a) $\dfrac{2}{5}x = 6$

(b) $\dfrac{3}{4}x = 5$

(c) $\dfrac{1}{7}x = -3$

(d) $\dfrac{2}{11}x = -4$

(e) $\dfrac{3}{8}x = -6$

(f) $-\dfrac{5}{7}x = -35$

ALGEBRA LINEAR EQUATIONS

2. Solve the following equations.

(a) $\dfrac{y+1}{3} = 6$

(b) $\dfrac{y+3}{4} = 5$

(c) $\dfrac{y+2}{5} = 4$

(d) $\dfrac{y+7}{3} = 2$

(e) $\dfrac{y+8}{2} = 6$

(f) $\dfrac{y+11}{4} = 12$

ALGEBRA LINEAR EQUATIONS

3. Solve the following equations.

(a) $\dfrac{3a + 6}{3} = -2$

(b) $\dfrac{3 - 3a}{6} = -5$

(c) $\dfrac{2a - 4}{6} = 3$

(d) $\dfrac{6 - 4a}{7} = -2$

(e) $\dfrac{4 + 6a}{2} = 8$

(f) $\dfrac{7a - 3}{9} = 2$

ALGEBRA LINEAR EQUATIONS

4. Solve the following equations.

(a) $\dfrac{3-2b}{3} = \dfrac{2}{5}$

(b) $\dfrac{2-3b}{4} = \dfrac{4}{5}$

(c) $\dfrac{6-2b}{9} = \dfrac{2}{5}$

(d) $\dfrac{7-b}{5} = \dfrac{3}{5}$

(e) $\dfrac{5-3b}{4} = -\dfrac{5}{6}$

(f) $\dfrac{7b+2}{12} = -\dfrac{3}{4}$

ALGEBRA LINEAR EQUATIONS

5. Solve the following equations.

(a) $\dfrac{3x - 2}{2} = \dfrac{4 - 8x}{3}$

(b) $\dfrac{6x - 1}{3} = \dfrac{2 - 3x}{4}$

(c) $\dfrac{x + 4}{4} = \dfrac{3 - 4x}{5}$

(d) $\dfrac{2x - 3}{6} = \dfrac{x + 1}{4}$

(e) $\dfrac{x + 2}{7} = \dfrac{6 - x}{3}$

(f) $\dfrac{3x - 2}{3} = \dfrac{2 - x}{6}$

ALGEBRA LINEAR EQUATIONS

6. Solve the following equations.

(a) $\dfrac{x+2}{2} + \dfrac{x-4}{3} = 1$

(b) $\dfrac{x+3}{3} - \dfrac{x-1}{4} = 1$

(c) $\dfrac{x+1}{4} - \dfrac{2x-1}{6} = 1$

(d) $\dfrac{2x+1}{3} - \dfrac{x+3}{2} = 2$

(e) $\dfrac{1-2x}{4} + \dfrac{2+3x}{3} = 2$

(f) $\dfrac{2-3x}{2} + \dfrac{x+1}{4} = 3$

ALGEBRA LINEAR EQUATIONS

7. Solve the following equations.

(a) $\dfrac{2x+1}{4} + \dfrac{3x+2}{3} = \dfrac{2}{3}$

(b) $\dfrac{x+5}{3} + \dfrac{x+2}{2} = \dfrac{1}{6}$

(c) $\dfrac{4x-2}{5} - \dfrac{2x+3}{4} = \dfrac{2}{5}$

(d) $\dfrac{x+2}{3} + \dfrac{5x-3}{2} = \dfrac{3}{4}$

(e) $\dfrac{3x-2}{6} + \dfrac{2x+3}{3} = \dfrac{10}{3}$

(f) $\dfrac{4x-1}{8} - \dfrac{2x-3}{2} = \dfrac{3}{4}$

ALGEBRA LINEAR EQUATIONS

6. Setting Up and Solving Linear Equations

Example :

In the following triangle, all angles are measured in degrees.

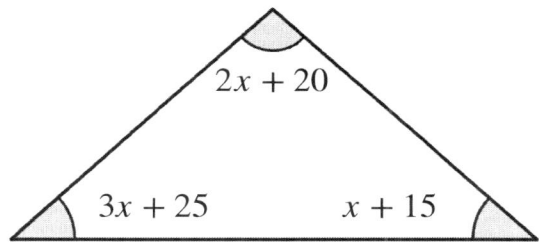

(a) Write down the expression in terms of x for the sum of the angles of the triangle.

(b) By setting up an equation, work out the value of x and the sizes of each angle.

Solution :

(a) $2x + 20 + x + 15 + 3x + 25 = 180$ The sum of the angles in a triangle is 180.

$6x + 60 = 180$

(b) $6x = 120$

$x = 20$

$2x + 20 = 2(20) + 20 = 60$

$x + 15 = 20 + 15 = 35$

$3x + 25 = 3(20) + 25 = 85$ The 3 angles are 35°, 60°, 85°.

ALGEBRA LINEAR EQUATIONS

Example :

Robert is 7 years older than Daniel. Alan is twice Daniel's age.

Suppose the total of their age is 39. Find the ages of Robert, Daniel and Alan.

Solution :

Let Daniel's age be x; then Robert's age is $x + 7$ and Alan's age is $2x$

$2x + x + x + 7 = 39$

$4x = 32$

$x = 8$ Hence, Daniel is 8 years old, Alan is 16, and Robert is 15.

Example :

A box of chocolates contains 3 flavours. There are the following numbers of each flavour:

Dark chocolate: $t + 3$ Vanilla chocolate: $2t + 5$ Strawberry chocolate: $3t - 6$

The total number of chocolates in a box is 44. Find the number of each flavour of chocolate.

Solution :

$t + 3 + 2t + 5 + 3t - 6 = 44$

$6t + 2 = 44$

$6t = 42$

$t = 7$

Hence, there are 10 dark chocolates, 19 vanilla chocolates and 15 strawberry chocolates.

ALGEBRA LINEAR EQUATIONS

Exercise 6:

1. The weight of 3 boxes is $y, 3y + 10, 5y + 20$.

(a) Write down the expression in terms of y for the total weight of the boxes.

(b) The total weight of the boxes is 75 kilograms. Find the weight of each box.

2. Dominic's maths score is 20 points higher than Marcus's. Marcus's maths score is 5% higher than Grace's. The total sum of their scores is 144. Find out Dominic's, Grace's and Marcus's scores.

3.

(a) Write down an expression in terms of x for the sum of the angles in the triangle below.

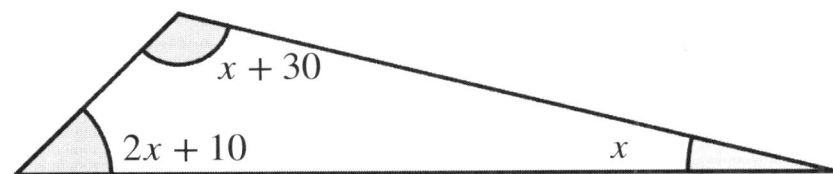

ALGEBRA LINEAR EQUATIONS

(b) Find the value of x

(c) Find the size of the largest angle of the triangle.

4. Bella is m years old. Emily is 4 times as old as Bella. In 6 years, Emily will be 34 years old. What is Bella's current age?

5. The sum of the angles in this shape is 540. Work out the size of the largest angle.

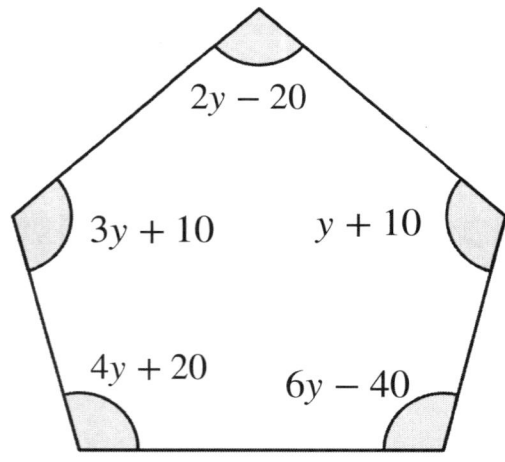

ALGEBRA LINEAR EQUATIONS

6. John lives x miles from Mary's house. He drives from his house to Mary's at an average speed of 40 mph. He drives back at an average speed of 35 mph. His total journey time is 6 hours.

(a) Write down an equation for the total time of the journey in terms of x.

(b) Solve the equation in part (a) to find out how far John lives from Mary's house.

7. A T-shirt costs y pounds. Peter bought a T-shirt and trousers. The trousers cost 3 times as much as the T-shirt. Peter paid £60 for the T-shirt and trousers.

(a) Write an equation for the total cost.

(b) Solve the equation in part (a) to find the cost of a T-shirt and trousers.

ALGEBRA LINEAR EQUATIONS

8. The perimeters of the 2 shapes in the following diagrams are equal.

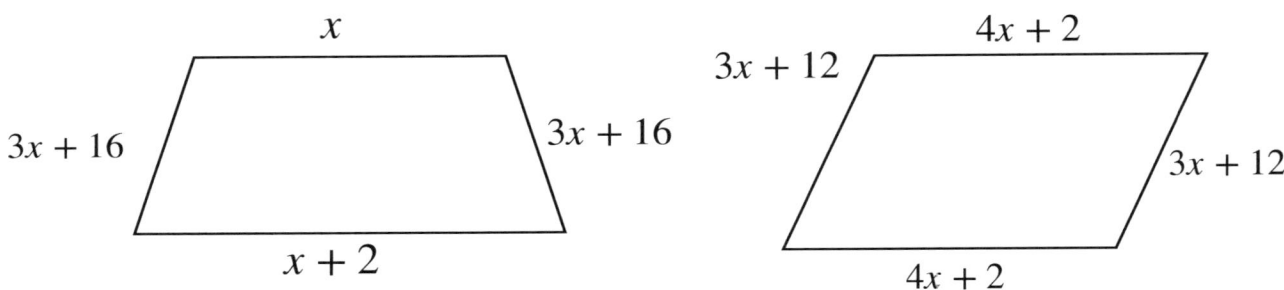

(a) Write down an equation in terms of x for the perimeter of the shapes.

(b) Solve the equation in part (a) to find the value of x.

9. David works for P hours each week for 5 weeks.

In the sixth week, he works for 4 hours less.

In the seventh week, he works for an extra 6 hours.

In the eighth week, he works for an extra 2 hours.

David works a total of 324 hours during these 8 weeks.

(a) Write down an equation in terms of P for the total hours he works.

(b) By solving the equation in part (a), find out the number of hours David worked in the eighth week.

10. The diagram shows a square and a rectangle.

All measurements are in centimetres. The perimeter of the square is equal to the perimeter of the rectangle.

(a) Write down an equation for the perimeter in terms of x.

(b) Work out the area of the rectangle.

ALGEBRA LINEAR EQUATIONS

ANSWERS

Exercise 1

1. (a) $a = 9$ (b) $x = 2\frac{1}{2}$ (c) $m = 2$ (d) $y = 8$ (e) $n = 6$ (f) $b = 4$

2. (a) $b = -7$ (b) $u = -4\frac{1}{2}$ (c) $-1\frac{5}{7}$ (d) $g = -4\frac{1}{2}$ (e) $m = -5$ (f) $y = -0.5$

3. (a) $y = -4$ (b) $p = -3$ (c) $m = -5$ (d) $g = -3$ (e) $n = -7$ (f) $n = -8$

4. (a) $y = -14$ (b) $t = -1$ (c) $n = -2$. (d) $m = 3$ (e) $p = 11$ (f) $q = 16$

5. (a) $g = 24$ (b) $a = 15$ (c) $b = 56$ (d) $y = -16$ (e) $d = 45$ (f) $t = 25$

Exercise 2

1. 48

2. 2

3. 49 years

4. 8:25am

5. $y = \dfrac{3x + 4}{4}$ or $y = \dfrac{3x}{4} + 1$

6. $x = 2\ y = 32$

Exercise 3

1. (a) $a = 3$ (b) $a = 4$ (c) $a = 3$ (d) $a = 7$ (e) $a = -\dfrac{1}{8}$ (f) $a = 2$

2. (a) $y = \dfrac{1}{2}$ (b) $y = 3\dfrac{1}{3}$ (c) $y = 2\dfrac{1}{5}$ (d) $y = -\dfrac{2}{3}$ (e) $y = \dfrac{1}{2}$ (f) $y = \dfrac{4}{5}$

ALGEBRA LINEAR EQUATIONS

3. (a) $y = -1\frac{1}{3}$ (b) $y = -7$ (c) $y = -1\frac{1}{3}$ (d) $y = -2$ (e) $y = -6$ (f) $y = -1$

4. (a) $b = \frac{1}{2}$ (b) $b = 1\frac{1}{3}$ (c) $b = -1$ (d) $b = \frac{2}{3}$ (e) $b = \frac{1}{2}$ (f) $b = \frac{7}{8}$

5. (a) $x = 7$ (b) $x = 2$ (c) $x = 2$ (d) $x = 6$ (e) $x = 2$ (f) $x = 3$

   (g) $x = -\frac{1}{4}$ (h) $x = -2$

Exercise 4

1. (a) $x = 2\frac{1}{4}$ (b) $x = -\frac{8}{9}$ (c) $x = -2\frac{1}{4}$ (d) $x = -5$ (e) $x = -6$ (f) $x = 1$

2. (a) $a = -7$ (b) $a = -\frac{3}{7}$ (c) $a = -2\frac{2}{3}$ (d) $-\frac{1}{10}$ (e) $a = 5$ (f) $a = 2\frac{5}{18}$

3. (a) $d = 3\frac{2}{3}$ (b) $d = 6\frac{1}{2}$ (c) $d = 3$ (d) $d = 2$ (e) $d = 17$ (f) $d = 2$

4. (a) $m = 10$ (b) $m = \frac{4}{7}$ (c) $m = 11$ (d) $m = -3$ (e) $m = 1\frac{9}{22}$ (f) $m = -6$

5. (a) $x = -10$ (b) $x = 3\frac{5}{7}$ (c) $x = 1\frac{5}{7}$ (d) $x = -\frac{22}{31}$ (e) $x = -\frac{9}{11}$ (f) $x = 4$

6. (a) $y = 14$ (b) $y = 4$ (c) $y = 6$ (d) $y = 6$ (e) $y = 3\frac{5}{22}$ (f) $y = 2\frac{2}{21}$

Exercise 5

1. (a) $x = 15$ (b) $x = 6\frac{2}{3}$ (c) $x = -21$ (d) $x = -22$ (e) $x = -16$ (f) $x = 49$

2. (a) $y = 17$ (b) $y = 17$ (c) $y = 18$ (d) $y = -1$ (e) $y = 8$ (f) $y = 37$

3. (a) $a = -4$ (b) $a = 11$ (c) $a = 11$ (d) $a = 5$ (e) $a = 2$ (f) $a = 3$

©Inspire Studies   Not to be copied

ALGEBRA LINEAR EQUATIONS

4. (a) $b = \dfrac{9}{10}$ (b) $b = -\dfrac{2}{5}$ (c) $b = 1\dfrac{1}{5}$ (d) $b = 4$ (e) $b = 2\dfrac{7}{9}$ (f) $b = -1\dfrac{4}{7}$

5. (a) $x = \dfrac{14}{25}$ (b) $x = \dfrac{10}{33}$ (c) $x = -\dfrac{8}{21}$ (d) $x = 9$ (e) $x = 3\dfrac{3}{5}$ (f) $x = \dfrac{6}{7}$

6. (a) $x = \dfrac{8}{5}$ (b) $x = -3$ (c) $x = -7$ (d) $x = 19$ (e) $x = 2\dfrac{1}{6}$ (f) $x = -\dfrac{7}{5}$

7. (a) $x = -\dfrac{1}{6}$ (b) $x = -3$ (c) $x = 5\dfrac{1}{6}$ (d) $x = \dfrac{19}{34}$ (e) $x = 2\dfrac{2}{7}$ (f) $x = 1\dfrac{1}{4}$

Exercise 6

1. (a) $9y + 30$ (b) 5kg, 25kg, 45kg

2. Grace : 40 marks; Marcus : 42 marks ; Dominic : 62 marks

3. (a) $4x + 40$ (b) 35 (c) 80

4. Bella is 7 years old

5. 170°

6. (a) $\dfrac{x}{40} + \dfrac{x}{35} = 6$ (b) $x = 112$ miles

7. (a) $4y = 60$ (b) T-shirt £15, Trouser £45

8. (a) $8x + 34 = 14x + 28$ (b) $x = 1$

9. (a) $8p + 4 = 324$ (b) 42 hours

10. (a) $8x + 16 = 10x + 10$ (b) $99\ cm^2$

ALGEBRA
LINEAR EQUATIONS

Also in this series :

Algebra fundamentals

Quadratic equations

Simultaneous equations

Printed in Great Britain
by Amazon

29637743R00026